DELILAH, EXCUSE ME!

JOSEPH SAYIBU

Unless otherwise indicated, all Scripture quotations are taken from the *Holy Bible, Authorized King James Version,* copyright ©2008 by Pilots Books, Hull, Georgia. All Rights Reserved.

Scripture marked NLT are taken from the *Holy Bible, New Living Translation,* copyright ©1996. Used by permission of Tyndale House Publishers, Inc., Wheaton, Illinois 60189. All Rights Reserved.

Scripture marked CEV is taken from the *Contemporary English Version.* Copyright ©1995 by the American Bible Society, New York, NY. Used by permission.

DELILAH EXCUSE ME

Copyright © 2015 by Joseph Sayibu

All rights reserved. No part of this book may be reproduced or transmitted in any form or by any means without written permission from the author.

ISBN: 1500482080
ISBN-13: 978-1500482084

For Speaking Engagement, Book Order and Comments
Please contact the author on:
Phone: +86 13841620371
WhatsApp Chat: +86 13841620371
https://www.facebook.com/josephsayibu
Email: josephsayibu1819@yahoo.co.uk

Dedication

To Abu E. Musah,

a man I admire

Acknowledgements

For the inspiration from, and to the reverence of Christ Jesus; the faithful witness, the Firstborn from the dead, the Ruler over the kings of the earth and to Him who loved us and washed us from our sins in His own blood.

I acknowledge with thanks, Pastor Mac Dunde, Head Pastor of the End-Time Redemption Assemblies of God Church, Gurugu-Tamale, Ghana, for building me up in the Lord by the various roles he assigned me in Church.

Special thanks to Silim-Babs Emelia, Kwame E. Nambu, Paul Kolbugri, Emmanuel Abaryate, and the Tamale Nurses' & Midwifery Training College (TNMTC) Chapter of the Assemblies of God Campus Ministry (AGCM) – Ghana.

I would also like to acknowledge and express my gratitude to the leadership and members of Jinzhou International Christian Fellowship (JICF),

China, for their generous sharing of wisdom, love, and fellowship.

My precious friend, Pascaline Enyonam Amanfu, for her love and support.

To all my manuscript reviewers, I say thank you for your valuable critiques in making this work a success.

May the good Lord bless you all for fuelling my Ministry in diverse ways.

Table of Contents

Introduction 9

1. The Strange Woman 17

2. Bitter Honeycombs 43

3. Don't Go Near Her Doors 53

4. Don't Give Away Your Honour 65

5. Drink From Your Own Well 73

6. Young Man, Cleanse Your Ways 83

7. Good News 95

About The Author 101

Introduction

HAPPY is the man that findeth wisdom, and the man that getteth understanding - (Proverbs 3:13). From the bosom of Solomon, the wisest of all men, came these words. Solomon had seen it all. He knew what benefit wisdom and understanding could give—a fulfilled life; a happy life.

Wisdom and understanding bring good life, long life and riches and honour. The Bible says, "Length of days is in her right hand; and in her left hand riches and honour" (Proverbs 3:16). Every young man needs to understand this. It is your responsibility to find wisdom and get understanding.

Delilah, Excuse Me!

Why? Because you're God's representative on earth; created in His own image, after His likeness. What this means is that you have in you, the Spirit of a God who has both wisdom and understanding as a character (Spirit): "And the spirit of the LORD shall rest upon him, the spirit of wisdom and understanding…" (Isaiah 11:2). And "the LORD by wisdom hath founded the earth; by understanding hath he established the heavens" (Proverbs 3:19).

Solomon discovered this truth and so, asked for nothing but wisdom and understanding when the Lord visited him.

Wisdom and understanding make you operate at a different dimension—a higher dimension. Solomon was operating at this level, so he could see and call others *"simple ones"*. He says, "And beheld among the simple ones, I discerned among the youths, a young man void of understanding" (Proverbs 7:7).

Life void of wisdom and understanding is naive. Get wisdom, get understanding: forget it not.

Introduction

Proverbs 14:18 says, "The simple inherit folly: but the prudent are crowned with knowledge." You would realize that it is more costly to stay simple. By the time you are through with this book you would discover how to find wisdom and get understanding.

"Wisdom is the principal thing; therefore get wisdom: and with all thy getting get understanding" (Proverbs 4:7), "that they may keep thee from the strange woman, from the stranger which flattereth with her words" (Proverbs 7:5).

"Delilah, Excuse Me! is fast becoming a cliché," the Lord whispered to me one day. This was one of the many slogans we adopted for our campus ministry (Assemblies of God Campus Ministry) in College, as coined by Ms. Emelia Silim-Babs, one of the first leaders of the local chapter of the ministry. Emelia had graduated when I became the leader and president of the chapter, and as the ministry grew, immoral sin on the College compound grew stronger and faster than anyone could predict. This

became so alarming that a national newspaper put up a story on my college with a heading I never did like: *"Sex Orgy in..."* I withhold the name of my College.

To protect the image of the ministry, the body of Christ, especially, the Holy Spirit led me to teach, and to organize teachings on topics such as holiness, purity, righteousness, grace and pardon for sin.

All this while, I could still hear the voice of God telling me, *"Delilah, Excuse Me!* is fast becoming a cliché." Now the Lord needed me to reach out to many youth all over the world with His message that was, and is hidden in our slogan: *Delilah, Excuse Me!* This book is therefore the message that the Lord hid in our slogan for us all.

Delilah, Excuse Me! is a book that brings wisdom and understanding to young men to keep them away from immoral women and immorality. Many young men lust after *"anything-in-a-skirt."* They are easily lured into gratifying their lust. Many oth-

Introduction

ers go into courtship without wisdom and understanding, and are led astray.

I have seen many *"youth-friendly"* books try to guide the youth in choosing and courting a mate. But those ideas or principles always have their shortcomings because they are only human ideas and principles. They always end up disappointing and hurting someone.

The only and surest way to know the right one to choose is to know the wrong one not to choose. You can only find a virtuous woman if you can identify and avoid a strange woman. If you agree with me, then, this book is the right material for you.

Although this book is directed toward young men, young women can as well benefit from it. The young woman would find equally useful, the message in this book, in her quest to becoming a virtuous woman, and to protect herself from the *"Jonadab"* and *"Amnon"* of our time (See 2 Samuel 13).

Delilah, Excuse Me!

"And it came to pass after this, that Absalom the son of David had a fair sister, whose name was Tamar; and Amnon the son of David loved her.

And Amnon was so vexed, that he fell sick for his sister Tamar; for she was a virgin; and Amnon thought it hard for him to do anything to her.

But Amnon had a friend, whose name was Jonadab, the son of Shimeah David's brother: and Jonadab was a very subtil man.

And he said unto him, Why art thou, being the king's son, lean from day to day? wilt thou not tell me? And Amnon said unto him, I love Tamar, my brother Absalom's sister.

And Jonadab said unto him, Lay thee down on thy bed, and make thyself sick: and when thy father cometh to see thee, say unto him, I pray thee, let my sister Tamar come, and give me meat, and dress the meat in my sight, that I may see it, and eat it at her hand.

So Amnon lay down, and made himself sick: and when the king was come to see him, Amnon said unto the king, I pray thee, let Tamar my sister come, and make me a couple of cakes in my sight, that I may eat at her hand.

Then David sent home to Tamar, saying, Go now to thy brother Amnon's house, and dress him meat.

So Tamar went to her brother Amnon's house; and he was laid down. And she took flour, and kneaded it, and made cakes in his sight, and did bake the cakes.

And she took a pan, and poured them out before him; but he refused to eat. And Amnon said, Have out all men from me. And they went out every man from him.

Introduction

And Amnon said unto Tamar, Bring the meat into the chamber, that I may eat of thine hand. And Tamar took the cakes which she had made, and brought them into the chamber to Amnon her brother.

And when she had brought them unto him to eat, he took hold of her, and said unto her, Come lie with me, my sister.

And she answered him, Nay, my brother, do not force me; for no such thing ought to be done in Israel: do not thou this folly.

And I, whither shall I cause my shame to go? and as for thee, thou shalt be as one of the fools in Israel. Now therefore, I pray thee, speak unto the king; for he will not withhold me from thee.

Howbeit he would not hearken unto her voice: but, being stronger than she, forced her, and lay with her.

Then Amnon hated her exceedingly; so that the hatred wherewith he hated her was greater than the love wherewith he had loved her. And Amnon said unto her, Arise, be gone.

And she said unto him, There is no cause: this evil in sending me away is greater than the other that thou didst unto me. But he would not hearken unto her.

Then he called his servant that ministered unto him, and said, Put now this woman out from me, and bolt the door after her.

And she had a garment of divers colours upon her: for with such robes were the king's daughters that were virgins apparelled. Then his servant brought her out, and bolted the door after her.

Delilah, Excuse Me!

And Tamar put ashes on her head, and rent her garment of divers colours that was on her, and laid her hand on her head, and went on crying."

2 Samuel 13:1-19

You will find Biblical principles to help you overcome the strategies of temptation by strange women around you.

Samson was seduced by a Philistine woman named Delilah (a woman of Sorek employed to discover the secret of Samson's strength in Judges 16:4-20). Her influence caused Samson to betray his special calling from God.

Samson, the mighty warrior, soon became a slave to his enemies.

Who is the Delilah in your life? This book is a warning: Beware of Seducers!

I pray that after reading this book, you will receive wisdom and understanding to stand up to her; look her in the face and say to her, *Delilah, Excuse Me!*

Chapter One

THE STRANGE WOMAN

For she hath cast down many wounded: yea, many strong men have been slain by her. Her house is the way to hell, going down to the chambers of death.

—*Proverbs 7:26-27*

A "STRANGE woman" is how the wisest of all men called her. "Her feet," he says, "abide not in her house." She lies in wait at every dark corner of the street. The book of Proverbs chapters 5 and 7 talk about her, the strange woman (an immoral woman).

Young man, hear me. Avoid her and live! "For she hath cast down many wounded: yea, many strong men have been slain by her. Her house is the way to hell, going down to the chambers of death" (Proverbs 7:26-27). Her victims are those who lack understanding. "But whoso committeth adultery with a woman lacketh understanding: he that doeth it destroyeth his own soul" (Proverbs 6:32).

There are two kinds of women that the book of Proverbs identifies—a *virtuous woman* and a *strange woman.*

The words of King Lemuel, the prophecy that his mother taught him in Proverbs 31:10-31 presents the virtuous woman.

Her price is far above rubies, and she does her husband good and not evil all the days of her life. Her children arise up, and call her blessed because she fears the Lord. Her mouth is full of wisdom and understanding, and in her tongue is the law of kindness. She surpasses all other capable women around her. She is a crown to her husband (Proverbs 12:4). Who can find such a woman? Lemuel asked. Proverbs says she is a good thing and comes with the favour of God. She is prudent and a gift from God.

The strange woman on the other hand, as King Solomon presents is vanity and a vexation of the spirit. She is crooked and cannot be made straight. She is as a jewel of gold in a swine's snout (Proverbs 11:22). To dwell in the wilderness is far better than with her; to dwell in the corner of the housetop is better than with her in a wide house. Her mouth is a deep pit (Proverbs 22:14); and she is always plucking down homes with her hands. She is as a continual dropping on a very rainy day (Proverbs 27:15). She is beautiful without godly character, thus, *"beastiful."*

In this book and chapter, I will be considering the strange woman. Our streets are still filled with strange women as in the Bible days; so, don't ask me what I'm talking about.

Today, they're no longer confined to obscure corners of the streets. They are everywhere: in our homes, neighbourhoods, offices, and even in the church.

Many Christian homes are broken, pastors seduced, and the young men sexually abused by the strange woman. She has wounded many, slain many more and has altogether destroyed their souls.

She is a dangerous foe to handle, young man. That is why you need wisdom and understanding. Wisdom and understanding will teach you that life is much more than eating to live, or living to eat.

"Life is a journey," it is said. But what many forget is this: life's journey, like any other has a destination and your task is to get there with a preserved soul. Everyone will surely finish this journey but the question is, with your soul in what condition, tattered or whole?

The Bible says, "but whoso committeth adultery with a woman lacketh understanding: he that doeth it destroyeth his own soul." The task of the

The Strange Woman

strange woman is to destroy your soul before you get to your destination.

Think of what your Maker will say to you when you present a tattered soul. Will your journey be worth celebrating and your arrival welcoming? Think about it!

Ask God to help you change your desires before you are drawn to sin. Remember, "she hath cast down many wounded: yea, many strong men have been slain by her. Her house is the way to hell, going down to the chambers of death." You are no exception without wisdom and understanding.

Samson was seduced by a Philistine woman named Delilah. Her influence caused Samson to betray his special calling from God. Samson, the mighty warrior, soon became a slave to his enemies.

I perfectly understand the *Growth-Sex Hormones factor;* if that is your argument. During the bloom of youth, sexual desires become strong. Powerful hormones are released that affect the reproductive organs. A youth thus becomes aware that these organs are capable of producing pleasurable sensations.

That you're under the influence of these hormones is no reason why you should destroy your soul. If the Science of hormonal activities is true then it's all part of God's handiwork, and thus under His control.

"But Joseph, the tension is always so great; you know it," one may say. "Tension can be an asset," says Carol Channing, the Broadway star, "if you make it work for you. It keeps you on your toes." Great truth!

The wet-dreams and early morning's erections you experience are no license for sexual promiscuity. They warn you that without understanding you might end up a father a kid-father. Don't add up to the increasing number of kids having kids!

How ever strong the influence of this hormonal activity in your body may be, wisdom and understanding, when they *"become members of your fam-*

The Strange Woman

ily" will guide your eyes and protect you from an affair with an immoral woman.

Sexual desires are of such importance that the Bible gives them special attention and counsels more careful restraint and self-control than with any other desire. Sex must be treated with great respect.

God has given us guidelines for the use of sex. The desire to violate these guidelines must be controlled. Sex, like fire, must be allowed in its rightful place. Fire is kept in the fireplace at home for warmth. When it's out of its rightful place it can burn down the whole house. So is sex out of its rightful place in our lives. It hurts; it destroys us and condemns us before our God.

"Women are like banks, boy, breaking and entering is a serious business," says British playwright Joe Orton.

Until you find wisdom and understanding, you will be vulnerable to the strange woman. It will be difficult to stand her sweet talk. She will wear you down completely with her kisses. "Her lips are as sweet as honey and her mouth is smoother than oil," the Bible says. Now that's a problem! How do you resist this package without wisdom and understanding?

If you were the young man Joseph in Potiphar's house, what would you have done?

Potiphar's wife was the strange woman in Joseph's home. "And it came to pass after these things, that his master's wife cast her eyes upon Joseph, and she said, Lie with me" (Genesis 39:7).

Here is poor Joseph, a slave being made an offer. Mrs. Potiphar was equally important and influential as her husband in the land of Egypt. Potiphar was an official of Pharaoh, a Captain. This should make his wife important.

"Lie with me" she said, "and I will give you all that you want; freedom, wealth, and promotion or anything, you just name it and it's all yours." Before young Joseph could say "you're my master's wife," she objected, "my husband, your master, is not at home. He's away on a long trip and won't return

The Strange Woman

until later this month." She would continue, "are you timid, or what else are you waiting for?" With the good council of wisdom and understanding, Joseph replied: "There is none greater in this house than I; neither hath he kept back anything from me but thee, because thou art his wife: how then can I do this great wickedness, and sin against God?" (Genesis 39:9).

Young Joseph was an honest man in a corrupt environment. He remained true and faithful to his master and to God despite the offer made him by a strange woman. This took him to prison. In a world like this, honesty kills; but its victims die more honourably. From prison, young Joseph became Prime Minister in a foreign land because of honesty.

Not until a young man realizes that sexual promiscuity is a sin against his own body, the body of the sexual partner, and above all, against God, he will destroy his own soul. The strange woman lies in wait for the young man void of understanding.

Joseph understood the limits. He knew that the bed of his master was not his territory. He purposed in his heart not to defile Potiphar's matrimonial bed, and so the Bible says "he fled, and got him out."

Joseph wasn't suffering any sexual dysfunction. He was a young man with sex hormones racing in his blood stream too. His androgen (testosterone) activity was no match for his wisdom and understanding.

Are you ready to flee also, from the strange woman? Then get wisdom and understanding. Get wisdom and understanding of what? Wisdom and understanding of God's original purpose of sexuality; understand that sex is God's gift to married people for their mutual enjoyment. If you want to have sex, then get married, young man! Married men should get this right—your freedom to sex is limited to your wife alone. Don't go in for other married women or single women. They will become the strange woman who will destroy your soul! Anyone who does this "lacketh understanding: he that doeth it destroyeth his own soul."

Alright, fine! So, who is this strange woman? How do I recognize her? Don't worry; Solomon, in Proverbs, answers that.

How Do I Recognize Her?

"Ye shall know them by their fruits… Wherefore by their fruits ye shall know them," Jesus told His disciples. The strange woman is astute and diverse in schemes. She is closely watching you. If you lack understanding, she will embrace you. Her lips are as sweet as honey and her mouth is smoother than oil. She has a flattering tongue. She is a consultant and an expert in flattery and smooth talk. She is loud and stubborn; nasty and cunning. She won't stop nagging until she traps you. The Bible tells of Delilah: "She tormented him with her nagging day after day until he was sick to death of it. Finally, Samson shared his secret with her" (Judges 16:16-17 NLT).

Her feet abide not in her house. She has developed a phobia for her own house. She is always found in the street soliciting at every corner. She loves the dark hours. "The eye also of an adulterer waiteth for the twilight, saying, No eye shall see me" (Job 24:15). Her visits are always at odd hours. She plans dates just for the two of you alone in the countryside, somewhere in the lonely woods. She has an excessive display of affection. She cherishes physical contact, hugging, petting, pecking, necking, kissing, fondling, and so on. She is a swinging door that easily opens up. She has no regard for morality. She speaks profanity. She lacks understanding. She is like one who says to God, "depart from me; for I desire not the knowledge of thy ways."

How Does She Operate?

Her strategies of temptation are very effective against the simple ones who lack wisdom and understanding. In Proverbs 7, Solomon warns us of

The Strange Woman

her operations and ways: "her ways are moveable, that thou canst not know them."

Though her schemes are many and varied, the Bible alerts us of these strategies so we will not be ignorant of her ways. Pay attention to the wise man and listen carefully to his wise counsel. Then you will show discernment, and your lips will express what you've learned.

1. She Looks For the Naive Young Men

She knows the unsuspecting young man will pass her way. It is said that "the devil finds work for idle hands to do." As Solomon was looking through his window one night he saw some naïve young men and one in particular who lacked common sense (Proverbs 7:7).

These young men lived their lives anyhow. They didn't seek wisdom and understanding. They only woke up every morning to live life just as it is. They practically followed the crowd. They didn't heed to the wise man's call to "get wisdom, get understanding: forget it not; neither decline from the words of my mouth." They were among the class of the simple ones; naïve and lacking common sense.

The person who has no purpose in life is naïve. The wise man saw among these naïve young men one in particular who lacked common sense. It will be safe to conclude that the rest were no different. It's often said that "birds of a feather flock together."

It was at twilight, in the evening, as deep darkness fell when these young men gathered outside without aim or direction.

It is true that "a person who is full refuses honey, but even bitter food tastes sweet to the hungry" (Proverbs 27:7 NLT). If you live an empty life, you will become more unstable and vulnerable to the tricks of the strange woman.

If you don't learn to set limits you won't have the sense to say, No! Avoid situations that could lead to sexual immorality. Keep an early curfew!

The Strange Woman

Wisdom and understanding will keep you far from an immoral woman. Those who hate wisdom love death. Foolishness will lead you straight to the door of her house. This fellow who lacked common sense went near the door of her house, graciously presenting himself as a living sacrifice. The wise man says, "passing through the street near her corner; and he went the way to her house" (Proverbs 7:8).

2. She Dresses To Allure Men

She has an attire of a harlot. She is seductively dressed. Her dressing has a great magnetic force, attracting young men void of understanding.

A woman's dressing speaks much of her. "A foolish woman is clamorous: she is simple, and knoweth nothing" (Proverbs 9:13).

Can you recount how Judah was deceived by his daughter-in-law's dressing? Genesis 38 holds the account. "And she put her widow's garments off from her, and covered her with a vail, and wrapped herself, and sat in an open place, which is by the way to Timnath; for she saw that Shelah was grown, and she was not given unto him to wife. When Judah saw her, he thought her to be an harlot; because she had covered her face" (Genesis 38:14-15).

This widow, Tamar, was Judah's daughter-in-law. Judah could recognize her in a modest outfit. But when she was seductively dressed, her charm blindfolded him and "he thought her to be an harlot."

The strange woman knows what turns you on. She is very much aware that what a man sees (sight) easily turns him on. So she makes your eyes her number one target. She draws your eyes' attention to herself by her dressing. Many ladies shamelessly expose their body to the public, all in the name of contemporary fashion. No, it's not about keeping pace with fashion; it's being a strange woman, a harlot!

Young man, understand this. She dresses to allure you. Beware of seducers; even in the Church. She exposes her breasts; she shows her abdomen, her thighs, her panties, and she dazzles you with a professional catwalk. She is a real top model. Sly of heart and seductively dressed, she's geared up for action. Avoid her! Job had this understanding, so he made a covenant with his eyes not to take a second look at the strange woman (Job 31:1). How about you?

3. Her Approach Is Bold

"...and she said, Lie with me" (Genesis 39:7). Potiphar's wife knew precisely what she wanted from Joseph. She went straight to the point. Lie with me. Her approach was clear-cut and bold. Delilah tormented Samson with her nagging day after day until he was sick to death of it. Finally, Samson shared his secret with her.

A strange woman's approach is bold and persistent. She will stop at nothing to pin you down.

Proverbs 7:13 says, "so she caught him, and kissed him." She cherishes physical contact hugging, petting, pecking, necking, kissing, fondling, and so on. She throws her hands around her victims and kisses them. Watch this! She initiates the physical intimacy. She is bold. That's her strength. It will only take a young man with wisdom and understanding to resist the warmth of her embrace.

4. She Invites You Over To Her Place

She doesn't stop at throwing her hands around you and kissing you, she invites you over to her house. Her house and bed are already in shape awaiting her prey. She prepares her bed ahead of time. This is why she is dangerous.

She watches you as she prepares herself, waiting for the opportunity to present itself. She won't miss the opportunity because she's well prepared ahead of time. She marks you in the daytime awaiting twilight. She rejoices when her plan is well executed: "I have peace offerings with me; this day have I payed my vows" (Proverbs 7:14).

The fellow who lacked common sense, as mentioned earlier was aimlessly strolling the street not knowing where he was going. He was unstable and vulnerable because he lacked a sense of purpose and

The Strange Woman

direction. He was tossed to and fro by circumstances around him. To him everything friends said was right was right.

Young man, listen to me and get understanding. The strange woman is able to discern a young man void of understanding. She knows where to find you. In verse 15 she says, "Therefore came I forth to meet thee... and I have found thee." She will take you to her house when she spots you. If you don't know where you're going, she will dictate your path. She has a place prepared for you. So get understanding and be saved.

5. She Cunningly Answers All Questions

Potiphar's wife was very smart. Before Joseph could say "you're my master's wife," she objected, "my husband, your master, is not at home. He's away on a long trip and won't return until later this month." That's how a strange woman cunningly answers all your questions and objections.

Ask her, what about your husband? She would say, "the goodman is not at home, he is gone a long journey: He hath taken a bag of money with him, and will come home at the day appointed" (Proverbs 7:19-20). She knows how long her husband would stay away. Now, tell her it's against Scripture and she would tell you how many Pastors do it. She would even allay your anxiety with verses from the Bible. "But 1 John 1:9 says 'if we confess our sins, he is faithful and just to forgive us our sins, and to cleanse us from all unrighteousness.' "

Object to her kiss and she would tell you it's a holy kiss. Tell her, "let's wait till we're married," and she would accuse you: "I thought you said you loved me; you're seeing another lady, I know… alright do it to prove your love for me!" Wisdom will teach you that love is different from, and far more than sexual attraction. She moves in with you before marriage and calls it *co-habitation.*

She always has an accurate response to your objection. Once you go near the door to her house, young man, your soul is prepared as a living sacrifice. "Prevention," they say, "is better than cure."

6. She Persuades You with Her Smooth Talk

Her smooth talk is captivating. "With her much fair speech she caused him to yield, with the flattering of her lips she forced him" (Proverbs 7: 21). Her lips are as sweet as honey and her mouth is smoother than oil. She knows what you're itching to hear. She tells you there's none else like you; you're the best. She sings to you the beautiful love Songs of Solomon. Her words are pleasant to the ear; they trap you. "...speak good words to them, they will be thy servants for ever" (2 Chronicles 10:7).

She mentions her bed is decked with coverings of tapestry, with carved works, with fine linen of Egypt; perfumed with myrrh, aloes, and cinnamon.

Expensive talk! This is enough to attract any man without understanding.

7. She Traps and Destroys You

She is extremely dangerous. She can destroy your family life. You will follow her like an ox going to the slaughter, and like a stag caught in a trap, awaiting the arrow that would pierce its heart.

She will degrade you. Humiliation is in her house and her bed is a store house of diseases. "For she hath cast down many wounded: yea, many strong men have been slain by her. Her house is the way to hell, going down to the chambers of death" (Proverbs 7:26-27). Her victims are those who lack understanding. "But whoso committeth adultery with a woman lacketh understanding: he that doeth it destroyeth his own soul" (Proverbs 6:32).

The wise man says in Proverbs 29:3 says, "Whoso loveth wisdom rejoiceth his father: but he that keepeth company with harlots spendeth his substance." He who hangs around with prostitutes wastes his wealth.

So listen to me, young man, don't gladly worship in her temple. Don't wander down her wayward path nor let your heart toward her.

The Preacher, after many years of searching and seeking out wisdom to understand the wicked-

The Strange Woman

ness of folly, even of foolishness and madness, found more bitter than death the woman whose heart is snares and nets, and her hands as bands (See Ecclesiastes 7:25-26). Only those that please God shall escape from her, but the sinner shall be taken by her. Avoid her and live!

If you are a young woman reading this book count yourself blessed. This special knowledge (wisdom and understanding) of fleeing sexual immorality will work for you too. It is for this reason that you have this revelation right now in your hands. Consider your ways and strive to be a real woman, a virtuous woman, like the Virgin Mary, consecrated and set apart for God's use. Ask yourself, who am I, a virtuous woman or a strange woman?

With King Solomon's picture of the strange woman, are you guilty of one or more of her characteristics? I could agree with you somewhat, that you're only keeping pace with contemporary fashion; that your dressing has nothing to do with alluring men. That is a good argument, innocent in itself. But the truth is that this innocent act is making someone "uncomfortable." That brother sitting next to you on the church's pew is disorientated by your outfit alone. His biochemical formula is altered with powerful hormones racing in his blood stream. He's now in a wonderland seeking the unspeakable, and not in the church. The brother in the street is empowered with *radioactive eyes* to make a mental picture of your nakedness. In his mind's eye you're naked without covering; and don't have him prosecuted when he rapes you.

Your innocent dressing might as well be harmful to brothers around you. Please do them a favour; dress modestly that they might not fall into temptation.

The Christian woman must not become a slave to the latest fashion at the expense of modesty. I'm not by this however, saying that your dressing should be catastrophic or that you should dress fifty years behind the current style. First Peter 3:3-4 ad-

The Strange Woman

vices: "Don't be concerned about the outward beauty of fancy hairstyles, expensive jewelry, or beautiful clothes. You should clothe yourselves instead with the beauty that comes from within, the unfading beauty of a gentle and quiet spirit, which is so precious to God" (NLT).

Think again; if what you do you do in the name of fashion, I urge you dear sister to redo it in the name of Christ.

Chapter Two

BITTER HONEYCOMBS

Someone asked Sophocles, 'How is your sex-life now? Are you still able to have a woman?' He replied, 'Hush, man; most gladly indeed am I rid of it all, as though I had escaped from a mad and savage master.'

—*Sophocles*

SAMSON gave a riddle in Judges 14. "Out of the one who eats came something to eat; out of the strong came something sweet," he said. The thirty young men from the town of Timnath answered the riddle after they had manipulated his wife to get the answer. They answered him: "What is sweeter than honey? What is stronger than a lion?"

Revelation 10:9 says, "…but it shall be in thy mouth sweet as honey." Honey is sweet, so are the lips of an immoral woman.

Many young men, like Samson have difficulty learning valuable lessons from past mistakes they've made. This unnamed wife of Samson, a woman in Timnath of the daughters of the Philistines in Judges Chapter fourteen double-crossed him with her false tears and nagging to tell the meaning of his riddle. This act of deceit led to a series of fatal encounters.

It appeared Samson didn't learn any lesson from this, when he went in again for another Philistine woman called Delilah. He should have known better when Delilah came up strong and determined to uncover the source of his strength. Samson, unfortunately, was carried away by the sweet words and smooth talk of a strange woman, and soon became a slave to his enemies.

All he needed do was to look her right in the face and say, *Delilah, excuse me!*

We today are no better with vital information. I hereby exhort you to be careful, young man, to whom you tell what.

A wise father told his son: "For the lips of a strange woman drop as an honeycomb, and her mouth is smoother than oil" (Proverbs 5:3). His son was excited; he wanted to meet this woman at once. "Young man, pay attention to the end of my tale before you set out to find her," the wise father told his son. He continued, "it's true her lips drop as an honeycomb but her end is bitter as wormwood, sharp as a two edged sword."

The Psalmist wrote of a deceitful man: "The words of his mouth were smoother than butter, but war was in his heart: his words were softer than oil, yet were they drawn swords" (Psalm 55:21). And

Delilah, Excuse Me!

John testifies; "…and it was in my mouth sweet as honey: and as soon as I had eaten it, my belly was bitter" (Revelation 10:10). She has a deceitful tongue; sweet as honey bitter as poison.

"What is sweeter than honey?" That is her bait. Young man, without understanding you will follow her like an ox going to the slaughter, and like a stag caught in a trap, awaiting the arrow that would pierce its heart.

The kisses of an enemy are deceitful! The strange woman is an enemy of your soul.

Sweet as honey, smoother than oil

Honey is stored in a honeycomb. A honeycomb is craftily built by bees to store honey. It's a collection of hexagonal cells constructed of wax. It serves as a nest in which honey is stored, eggs are laid, and larvae developed.

The truth is that if you dip your hand into a beehive for honey, you might as well come out with a bee sting that might kill you. So, you see, honeycombs do not only hold sweet honey, they house deadly bee stings as well.

The lips of the immoral woman are as sweet as honey, and her mouth is smoother than oil. Her smooth talk is her charm. Her sweet talk is tempting. "Pleasant words are as an honeycomb, sweet to the soul, and health to the bones" (Proverbs 16:24). She sounds so romantic "I've perfumed my bed with myrrh, aloes, and cinnamon. Come; let's drink our fill of love until morning. Let's enjoy each other's caresses."

Her smooth talk is captivating and the kiss of her lips is irresistible. "With her much fair speech she caused him to yield, with the flattering of her lips she forced him" (Proverbs 7: 21). Her lips are as sweet as honey and her mouth is smoother than oil. She knows what you're itching to hear. She tells you there's none else like you; you're the best. She sings to you the love Songs of Solomon. Her words are pleasant to the ear; they trap you. "…speak good words to them, they will be thy servants for ever" (2 Chronicles 10:7).

She mentions her bed is decked with coverings of tapestry, with carved works, with fine linens of Egypt; perfumed with myrrh, aloes, and cinnamon. Expensive talk! This is enough to attract any man without understanding.

Bitter as wormwood, sharp as a two edged sword

"But her end is bitter as wormwood, sharp as a two edged sword. Her feet go down to death; her steps take hold on hell" (Proverbs 5:4-5). The after-effects of sexual sin are devastating. Imagine the heartache if years later one realized that a sexual experience has caused irreversible damage, perhaps infertility or a serious health problem.

You will groan in your future when your flesh and your organism come to an end. The wise man didn't hide that: "And thou mourn at the last, when thy flesh and thy body are consumed" (Proverbs 5:11).

It will be too late to seek wisdom and understanding when you face her poison. Remember, "Bread of deceit is sweet to a man; but afterwards his mouth shall be filled with gravel" (Proverbs 20:17).

She said, "I have peace offerings with me..." but Proverbs 21:27 disagrees with her: "The sacrifice of the wicked is abomination: how much more, when he bringeth it with a wicked mind."

"The words of his mouth were smoother than butter, but war was in his heart: his words were softer than oil, yet were they drawn swords," says the Psalmist. All is not gold that glitters. All is not good that taste sweet. She is vanity and vexation of the spirit; a two-edged sword destroying both body and soul. We are cautioned in Proverbs 16:25; "There is a way that seemeth right unto a man, but the end thereof are the ways of death."

"And the name of the star is called Wormwood: and the third part of the waters became wormwood; and many men died of the waters, because they were made bitter" (Revelation 8:11). John the Revelator tells of a great star that fell from heaven, when the third angel sounded his trumpet. Burning as it were like a lamp it fell upon the third part of the rivers, and upon the fountains of waters. That star was wormwood.

Her presence in the third part of the rivers and upon the fountains of waters made the very wholesome waters thereafter, bitter and poisonous. Every man drinking of the waters, unsuspecting, died of poisoning.

The strange woman though sparkling is poisoned with wormwood, which is why she is dangerous. Her end thereof is the way of death.

She is a swinging door that easily opens up for her guests to cross over to hell.

She's a one-way transit; only an entry not an exit. Once you enter, you're on your way down to the chambers of death. It's a journey of no return! "For she hath cast down many wounded: yea, many strong men have been slain by her. Her house is the way to hell, going down to the chambers of death" (Proverbs 7:26-27).

She is bitter as wormwood, and sharp as a two-edged sword! Her peace offering is an abomination to the Lord.

Chapter Three

DON'T GO NEAR HER DOORS

In the spring a young man's fancy lightly turns to what he's been thinking about all winter.

—Cary Grant

OBEY the Bible's admonition: "Now the body is not for fornication, but for the Lord; and the Lord for the body. Flee fornication. Every sin that a man doeth is without the body; but he that committeth fornication sinneth against his own body" (1 Corinthians 6:13&18).

Delilah, Excuse Me!

"How is fornication a sin against my own body?" one may ask. You'll understand it better if years later you realized that a sexual experience had caused irreversible damage, perhaps infertility or a serious health problem. You will groan in your future when your flesh and your organism come to an end, when deadly diseases consume your body.

The door to her house is welcoming, "but her end is bitter as wormwood, sharp as a two edged sword. Her feet go down to death; her steps take hold on hell" (Proverbs 5:4-5). The aftereffects of sexual sin are devastating.

Better it is, though, to avoid sexual immorality! Do not be fooled by those who say you can get away with it. God is not mocked, what you sow, you shall reap also.

The wise father warns: "Hear me now therefore, O ye children, and depart not from the words of my mouth. Remove thy way far from her, and come not nigh the door of her house" (Proverbs 5:7-8).

Don't Go Near Her Doors

If you don't learn to set limits you won't have the sense to say, No! Avoid situations that could lead to her door, sexual immorality. Keep an early curfew! Wisdom and understanding will keep you far from an immoral woman. Those who hate wisdom love death. Foolishness will lead you straight to the door of her house.

This fellow who lacked common sense went near the door of her house, graciously presenting himself as a living sacrifice. The wise man says, "passing through the street near her corner; and he went the way to her house" (Proverbs 7:8).

"Keep busy," exhorts teen writer Esther Davidowitz. Find wisdom and get understanding. "Evil comes at leisure like the disease; good comes in a hurry like the doctor," says British writer and poet, G. K. Chesterton. Take up a hobby, do some exercise, begin a Bible research project, or study a language. Staying engrossed in useful activities can keep you from going near doors of strange women.

Delilah, Excuse Me!

Late one afternoon, after his midday rest, David got out of bed and was idling on the roof of the palace. It was spring when kings normally go out to war. However, David stayed behind in Jerusalem. He abandoned his purpose and work by staying home from war, focusing on his own desires.

David's adultery with Bathsheba could have been averted had he kept busy and gone out to war. Maybe Bathsheba was rash in bathing where she might be seen. But in any case, David should have been at war with his army. Always keep busy for the devil finds work for idle hands to do.

Her door never closes. She's always operational. She keeps busy decorating and disguising it all day long. On her door you'll see this inscription, boldly written: *"I've perfumed my bed with myrrh, aloes, and cinnamon. Come; let's drink our fill of love until morning. Let's enjoy each other's caresses."* Her invitations are to the simple ones void of understanding.

The Bible says, "she sitteth at the door of her house, on a seat in the high places of the city, to call passengers who go right on their ways" (Proverbs 9:14-15). She sits in her doorway on the heights overlooking the city. "Come in with me," she urges the simple, and to those who lack understanding, she says, "stolen water is refreshing; food eaten in secret tastes the best."

Purpose in Your Heart Not To Defile Yourself

Young Daniel was determined not to defile himself by eating the food and wine given to them by King Nebuchadnezzar. He didn't eat of the king's portion not because it wasn't good enough. Remember these were special meals with royal taste, carefully weighed to provide every nutrient in its right quantity and proportion. These were delicious and well balanced meals provided free of charge. But Daniel, we read from the Bible, resisted these royal banquet treats because he purposed in his heart not to defile himself. Can you resist a free offer from the strange woman? Are you ready to purpose in your heart not to defile yourself? Will you gladly miss that "perfect opportunity" for sex? Will you stand out against all odds? Like Daniel, you can! You can equally make God proud of you, like Job.

Don't let your heart stray away toward a strange woman, young man. Don't wander down her corner in the street. Stay focused and be purposeful. Learn to say no, and mean it. Don't let her coy glances seduce you nor lust after her beauty. She will bring you to poverty and cost you your life. "For by means of a whorish woman a man is brought to a piece of bread: and the adultress will hunt for the precious life" (Proverbs 6:26).

Dear young man, the Scripture in Colossians 3:5 forcefully state this: "Have nothing to do with sexual immorality, impurity, lust, and evil desires" (NLT).

Don't Go Near Her Doors

Many mighty men have dared to tread the path to her doorway, and have paid dearly. Many more never found their way out of her house. They all were led as an ox going to the slaughter, and like a stag caught in a trap, awaiting the arrow that would pierce its heart.

The young man in Proverbs chapter 7 could have avoided the door of the strange woman had he kept good company instead. Solomon saw a company of naïve young men in the street that evening. They were the simple, lacking understanding.

In Psalm 119:63, the Psalmist declared: "I am a companion of all them that fear thee, and of them that keep thy precepts." The precepts of the Lord bring good judgment and knowledge (Psalm 119:66). Who are your friends? Keep friends who strive to keep God's orders. If you are around people who love the Lord, you find that, as you talk about morals, you start to feel the same way they do. For instance, if you hear them say immorality is disgusting, you begin to feel likewise. On the other hand, if you're with someone that doesn't care, pretty soon you'll become just like him. "He that walketh with wise men shall be wise: but a company of fools shall be destroyed" (Proverbs 13:20).

Guard your soul, young man. Realize the folly of passing through the street near her corner, and going near the door of her house.

Remember that small wrong decisions often lead to big mistakes. Save your soul, "for she hath cast down many wounded: yea, many strong men have been slain by her. Her house is the way to hell, going down to the chambers of death."

The LORD'S judgment came against Nineveh again in the book of Nahum chapter three. The people of Nineveh had returned to their sin, after their repentance at Jonah's preaching. Nineveh had used its beauty, prestige, and power to seduce other nations into false friendships. Then when the other nations relaxed, thinking Nineveh was a friend, she would attack and plunder them. This is exactly what every strange woman does. Like Nineveh, strange

Don't Go Near Her Doors

women appear beautiful and impressive on the outside, but vicious and deceitful on the inside.

Don't let her seduce you into lowering your standards or compromising your moral principles. Beneath her attractive façade lies seduction and death.

Love wisdom like a sister; make understanding your kinswoman. They will keep you from the doors of strange women. Don't defile yourself!

Make a Covenant with Your Eyes

The Old Testament law said that it was wrong for a person to have sex with someone other than your spouse. But Jesus said that the desire to have sex with someone other than your spouse is mental adultery and thus sin. If the act is wrong, then so is the intention. Hear Jesus in Matthew 5:28; "But I say, anyone who even looks at a woman with lust has already committed adultery with her in his heart" (NLT).

Both the intention and the act are condemned. You might be legally innocent, but morally guilty. The intention or desire leads to the act and thus is sin. The desire is the starting point of every sexual sin. Lust is the problem not the look.

In Job's final protest of innocence, he tells us: "I made a covenant with my eyes not to look with lust at a young woman" (Job 31:1 NLT). Job protested his innocence of sexual sin among others. He wasn't guilty of sexual sin because he had discovered the one vital secret to avoiding sexual sin, not to look with lust at a young woman.

It is not just enough to discover this very secret. You will need to work it out. Like Job, you may need to make a covenant with your eyes. Had David made a covenant with his eyes, he would have closed them on this woman of unusual beauty (Bathsheba) taking a bath.

The eyes in the same manner as the heart must be guarded diligently. For whatever the eyes see the heart paints. What you see is painted on the tablets

Don't Go Near Her Doors

of your heart, leaving a clear picture in your mind. Your mind keeps nurturing and desiring it. Your whole being is corrupted seeking to gratify this evil desire. If this process is not interrupted, sexual sin is inevitable.

You cannot blame anyone for your temptation and sin. The Scripture is very clear on this in James 1:13-15: "Let no man say when he is tempted, I am tempted of God: for God cannot be tempted with evil, neither tempteth he any man: but every man is tempted, when he is drawn away of his own lust, and enticed. Then when lust hath conceived, it bringeth forth sin: and sin, when it is finished, bringeth forth death."

Looking at a woman lustfully is the very beginning of a sexual act. This is why pornographic materials have become the single most powerful and deadly weapon that the devil uses to destroy young people today. Today, pornography is everywhere: you walk down the street and there it is displayed openly on newsstands. Erotic movies, books and magazines, internet, and television shows have compounded the problem.

Pornography is mentally corrupting. It makes it difficult enough to focus on things that are chaste and praiseworthy. The eyes are the window to the heart and mind. Whatever the eyes see, be sure to have a painting of it in the mind and heart. So, one way to guard the heart is to guard the eyes.

Chapter Four

DON'T GIVE AWAY YOUR HONOUR

Only one man in a thousand is a leader of men—the other 999 follow women.

– *Groucho Marx*

IF you go near the door of her house, you will lose your honour. "Remove thy way far from her, and come not nigh the door of her house: Lest thou give thine honour unto others, and thy years unto the cruel: Least strangers be filled with thy wealth; and thy labours be in the house of a stranger; And thou mourn at the last, when thy flesh and thy body are consumed, And say, How have I hated instruction, and my heart despised reproof; And have not obeyed the voice of my teachers, nor inclined mine ear to them that instructed me! I was almost in all evil in the midst of the congregation and assembly" (Proverbs 5:8-14).

Honour is personal integrity; dignity; respect and reputation—so you may call it. However we see it, it all narrows down to having a renowned reputation or social standing; physical or spiritual blessings (from God) and merited respect. Preserving it is as important as earning it. Honour is an extremely valuable asset not to be given away cheaply. The wise would protect it with their lives. A Vietnamese proverb says: "Better die in honour than live in disgrace." I agree. It's far better to die holding on to your honour than to continue living in disgrace, dishonour, and stigma. The wise father agrees also when he warns; "Lest thou give thine honour unto others, and thy years unto the cruel."

Choose to be the one man leading men, and not the other 999 men following women. Some don't just follow women, but strange women. Why follow women whose houses are the way to hell, going down to the chambers of death? When a strange woman leads you, you will follow her like an ox going to the slaughter, and like a stag caught in a trap, awaiting the arrow that would pierce its heart.

"Wisdom," the Bible says, "is the principal thing." Embrace therefore, wisdom, and she will bring you honour (Proverbs 4:8). Embrace folly, and she will lead you to the doors of a strange woman. At the door of her house your honour shall be taken away from you. You will lose it to strangers. You will lose it to the cruel that eat "stolen bread" in the inner chambers of her house. They are the simple ones void of understanding, having no need of honour. "There is no honour among thieves," goes an old adage.

Young man, I warn you to stay far from her doors, remove your foot from evil, lest you lose your honour. It is not passé to keep your virginity! It should make you proud, because it is rare. Only an exceptional young man is able to travel through adolescence and remain a virgin. Friends mock your chastity simply because they've lost their honour, and are jealous of you. You are no freak! Be bold and keep your honour. Be the real you, and don't try to be your friends. "I'll wager you that in 10 years it will be fashionable again to be a virgin," says Barbara Cartlan. Be a part of this transformation. Trying to please everyone is a key to failure in life. So, be you, and live as you.

Mildred Newman and Bernard Berkowitz in their book, *How to Take Charge of your Life,* write of Sosya: *One day, a great teacher named Sosya, ripe with years and honours, lay dying. His students and disciples asked if he was afraid to die. "Yes," he said. "I'm afraid to meet my Maker." "How can that be? You have lived such an exemplary life. You have led us out of the wilderness of ignorance, like Moses. You have judged between us wisely, like*

Solomon." Sosya replied: "When I meet my Maker, He will not ask, 'Have you been like Moses or Solomon?' "He will ask, 'Have you been Sosya?!' "

Have you been you? Or you've been your friends? Maybe it is time to introduce yourself to you. Know yourself, and be you! Don't just follow the crowd; get wisdom, get understanding.

Flee fornication. "But put ye on the Lord Jesus Christ, and make not provision for the flesh, to fulfil the lusts thereof" (Romans 13:14). Work out this with passion and gusto. Guard your heart with all diligence and give no room to sexually stimulating materials which whips up "sexual appetite." Ponder instead on things that are chaste and clean. Philippians 4:8 admonishes the Christian to consciously guide his thoughts: "Finally, brethren, whatsoever things are true, whatsoever things are honest, whatsoever things are just, whatsoever things are pure, whatsoever things are lovely, whatsoever things are of good report; if there be any virtue, and if there be any praise, think on these things."

Joseph held on to his honour and it brought him promotion; he heeded the voice of wisdom and regarded understanding. Conversely, Samson gave away his honour and was reduced to a piece of bread for his enemies to trample upon. Esau had to pay so dearly for his folly when he traded his honour (birthright) for a bowl of soup.

Young man, listen to me, don't trade your soul, birthright, and honour to the devil for a strange woman. Wisdom is your sister, remember? So, be wise! "If you become wise, you will be the one to profit. If you scorn wisdom, you will be the one to suffer" (Proverbs 9:12 NLT).

"Remove thy way far from her, and come not nigh the door of her house: Lest thou give thine honour unto others, and thy years unto the cruel: Least strangers be filled with thy wealth; and thy labours be in the house of a stranger; And thou mourn at the last, when thy flesh and thy body are consumed, And say, How have I hated instruction, and my heart despised reproof; And have not obeyed the voice of my teachers, nor inclined mine ear to them that instructed me! I was almost in all evil in the midst of the congregation and assembly."

Imagine how much of one's fortune one would lose to pharmaceutical companies, all in the name of undergoing an Anti-retroviral Therapy. Consider the public stigma, disgrace, pain, disappointment, and frustration you would have to contend with for the rest of your life. Consider the grief and depression when your doctors throw their hands up in despair and whisper to you, "sorry, there's nothing more we can do." When all hope is gone and you're declared a moribund patient on your sick bed, then you'll mourn and say, "How have I hated instruction, and my heart despised reproof; And have not obeyed the voice of my teachers, nor inclined mine ear to them that instructed me!" It will be rather too late to seek wisdom and understanding on this day when your body is consumed by a deadly disease. The right time to seek wisdom and understanding is now.

Chapter Five

DRINK FROM YOUR OWN WELL

A wife at home is worth two in the street.

MARRIAGE is not a cure to sexual promiscuity; it is wisdom and understanding. Stop it now, or you'll make an unfaithful husband. Young man, don't be deceived. Promiscuity is not a trademark of youthfulness neither is marriage a cure to promiscuity. The truth is that a promiscuous person lacks understanding, and not because he or she

Delilah, Excuse Me!

is a youth. If you don't learn to discipline yourself when you are still single, you won't when you are married! Hear what the Scripture says; "But whoso committeth adultery with a woman lacketh understanding: he that doeth it destroyeth his own soul" (Proverbs 6:32). Just because you are married does not mean there are no more women out there. So if you couldn't restrain yourself before you were married, you will not restrain yourself after you are married. The same temptation will continue to present itself; and if you couldn't overcome it yesterday, you definitely will not overcome it today. Say no to sexual promiscuity!

The Bible is not against sex, but against sexual perversion. Where do you draw the line between both? The Bible, in the book of Hebrews 13:4, says, "Marriage is honourable in all, and the bed undefiled: but whoremongers and adulterers God will judge." The marriage bed is what rejoices God. It's only on this bed, that sex is pure and pleasant to God. There's no defilement on this bed! It's pure and acceptable in the Lord's sight. It's a glorious act!

That's where He draws the line. Any other bed other than the marriage bed—any other form or means of sexual relation is sexual perversion; and God will judge.

The Bible everywhere celebrates heterosexual, monogamous marriage as the proper situation for sexual fulfillment. Christian men and women should be open to true love and to sexual intimacy within the commitment to lifelong fidelity. That is God's way. The rest is dangerous and futile. "Profanation and violation are part of the perversity of sex, which never will conform to liberal theories of benevolence. Every model of morally or politically correct sexual behaviour will be subverted, by nature's daemonic law", says Camille Paglia.

Sexual sin and perversion will drain your energies and turn your heart away from God.

When the apostle Paul was confronted with this issue he wrote back to the church in Corinth saying this: "Now concerning the things whereof ye wrote unto me: It is good for a man not to touch a woman.

Delilah, Excuse Me!

Nevertheless, to avoid fornication, let every man have his own wife, and let every woman have her own husband" (1 Corinthians 7:1-2). Fornication was becoming an issue in the church just as today, so, in order that every man and woman would satisfy their sexual appetite rightly, Paul advised them (and us too) to marry and stay faithful. He continued; "The husband should fulfill his wife's sexual needs, and the wife should fulfill her husband's needs. The wife gives authority over her body to her husband, and the husband gives authority over his body to his wife. Do not deprive each other of sexual relations" (NLT). This, I think, should solve the problem.

Both marriage and singleness are gifts from God (1 Corinthians 7:7). Both are morally important and right. But if you cannot preserve your body for God, please marry, young man. And when you marry, stay by your own well and drink only from your own well. Proverbs 5:15 says: "Drink waters out of thine own cistern, and running waters out of thine well." Why leave the refreshing waters from your own cistern and well, and take to the street? You will be charged for stealing water out of another's well. Save yourself this embarrassment.

"Drink waters out of thine own cistern... out of thine well" is a perfect picture of faithfulness in marriage. Young man, enjoy your wife. By her you'll obtain favour from God.

Let Thy Fountain Be Blessed

Zip up, young man! Why spill the water of your springs in the street, having sex with just anyone in a skirt? Safeguard your fountain; reserve it and don't share it with strangers. "Let thy fountains be dispersed abroad, and rivers of waters in the streets. Let them be only thine own, and not strangers' with thee" (Proverbs 5:16-17). The New Living Translation (NLT) puts it this way: "Why spill the water of your springs in the streets, having sex with just anyone? You should reserve it for yourselves. Never share it with strangers."

Stay chaste and pure; for a day is coming when a beautiful bride shall thirst for water out of your fountain. Will your fountain be called "blessed?" Will your "rivers of waters" be refreshing?

Your fountain cannot hold both refreshing waters and bitter waters. Don't contaminate your fountain of refreshing waters. James 3:11-12 inquires, "Doth a fountain send forth at the same place sweet water and bitter?" He answers no, and says, "...so can no fountain both yield salt water and fresh." Please get this right, young man. Your fountain must be kept safe, free from contamination; it must be of refreshing waters. Your offspring shall be like the tree in Psalm 1:3, a tree planted by the rivers of water, that bringeth forth his fruit in his season; his leaf also shall not wither; and whatsoever he doth shall prosper. But the offspring of a bitter and salty fountain shall be rooted out. They are like the chaff which the wind driveth away.

Don't disperse your fountain abroad, bring it home! Don't share it in the streets to just "anything-in-a-skirt." Remember, strange women lie in wait to seize your blessings and your honour. Don't carelessly pursue sexual pleasures and miss out on God's blessings. Let thy fountain be blessed!

Rejoice With the Wife of Thy Youth

Sex is a gift from God to married people. It's for their mutual enjoyment. God really never intended married life to be boring, dull, and lifeless. Sexual union means oneness and total knowledge of the other person. Sexual intercourse is the most intimate of acts, sealing a social, physical, and spiritual relationship. That is why God has reserved it for marriage alone.

Love and cherish your wife. She's the good thing you found. Rejoice with her and her alone! Ecclesiastes 9:9 clearly states this: "Live joyfully with the wife whom thou lovest all the days of the life of thy vanity, which he hath given thee under the sun, all the days of thy vanity: for that is thy portion in this life, and thy labour which thou takest under the sun."

"Why be captivated, my son, by an immoral woman, or fondle the breasts of a promiscuous woman?" (Proverbs 5:20 NLT). If your wife is not good at *"hardcore,"* then go *"softcore."* If you feel impotent or can no longer maintain your erection in your wife's presence, seek medical help or talk to a sex therapist. Be wise to discern, and excuse any *"holy spirit"* that tells you to divorce your wife! Our God is not a God of confusion (1 Corinthians 14:33). You'll have no excuse before God.

If you would listen to me, I would tell you a wife at home is worth two in the street. "Marriage is honourable in all, and the bed undefiled: but whoremongers and adulterers God will judge" (Hebrews 13:4). Remember your marriage vow: "Till death do us part!" The Lord was a witness. You'll have no business in the streets near the doors of a

Drink From Your Own Well

strange woman. She will take your honour and destroy your soul.

Don't think you're covered. The Lord sees clearly what a man does, and examines every path he takes. An evil man is held captive by his own sins; they are ropes that catch and hold him.

Young man, you'll die for lack of self-control. You will be lost because of your great foolishness! Give up your simple ways and embrace wisdom. Let understanding be a part of you.

You will groan and God will not hear you because of your marital unfaithfulness. "Yet ye say, Wherefore? Because the LORD hath been witness between thee and the wife of thy youth, against whom thou hast dealt treacherously: yet is she thy companion, and the wife of thy covenant" (Malachi 2:14).

Let the breasts of your wife satisfy you always. She is a loving deer; a graceful doe. Be captivated by her love (Proverbs 5:19). Learn to remain faithful and true to her even in your old age because she is the wife of your youth. She is your portion in this life. Drink from your own well!

Chapter Six

YOUNG MAN, CLEANSE YOUR WAYS

Lord, forgive me if my need

Sometimes shapes a human creed.

—Countee Cullen

IN Psalm 119:9, the psalmist posed a question: "Wherewithal shall a young man cleanse his way?" The answer: "by taking heed thereto according to thy word." Young man, I know often times

Delilah, Excuse Me!

you've asked similar questions like the psalmist's. Our world is so contaminated with sin. Every day presents us with diverse temptation. Everywhere we look we find temptation to fill our minds with thoughts of sexual relations that God wouldn't approve of. Turn on the television, and you will see horrible sexual images; pick up a newspaper or magazine, and you will see sexual images and read profane articles. The number one hit-tracks on air project nothing useful but sex; the lyrics are profane. One is always in danger of sinful attraction. Look around you, and it seems everyone else is doing it except you. Your peers keep calling you names you don't like. The pressure is just too great to bear. Then you'll ask yourself how do I stay pure in a world like this? This one question troubles us all, so you're not alone.

The Psalmist closely followed his question with an answer, seeing how important the question was. Now we have a way out; we can stay pure in a cor-

Young Man, Cleanse Your Ways

rupt environment. How? "By taking heed thereto according to thy word," the Psalmist says.

The word of God is the only guide for righteous living, which is why you need it in your daily walk through this world. Study the scriptures and memorize them and apply them to your life. The word of God will be a lamp to guide your feet and a light for your path. To walk safely through this corrupt world you'll need the light of God's Word to see clearly.

As you read the Bible, be alert for lessons, commands, or examples that you can apply to your life. The scriptures you learn only become effective when put into practice. A successful Christian life is gained by the practical application of God's Word.

Young man, the strange woman will destroy your soul if you don't live according to God's ordinances. Always remember God's advice to Joshua in Joshua 1:8: "This book of the law shall not depart out of thy mouth; but thou shalt meditate therein day and night, that thou mayest observe to do according to all that is written therein: for then thou shalt make thy way prosperous, and then thou shalt have good success."

Young man, cleanse your ways. Stay away from sexual immorality and from strange women. Keep your ways pure. Repent, and receive grace and pardon for a new life, a life with purpose. Allow God to create in you a clean heart and renew a loyal spirit within you (Psalm 51:10). God is able to forgive all your wrong doings and clear all of your guilt. He will cleanse you from within of all your mistakes. Enough is enough! It's time to say No to sexual immorality, and to recover all your honour. It's time to say, *Delilah, Excuse Me!* She's had enough of you. It's time to break loose. Young man, it's show time!

Do you genuinely want to stop? Are you really sorry for your sins? If you answer yes, then know that God is pleased with you. Remember, God can and will forgive sexual sin just as He forgives other sins. Start by asking Him to create in you a pure heart and spirit. A pure heart and spirit guarantees right conduct. It imbues you with wisdom and understanding from Heaven.

Zip Up!

Young man, keep your zip up at all times. Zip up, young man! Why spill the water of your springs in the street, having sex with just anyone in a skirt? Safeguard your fountain; reserve it and don't share it with strangers. "Let thy fountains be dispersed abroad, and rivers of waters in the streets. Let them be only thine own, and not strangers' with thee" (Proverbs 5:16-17). Don't carelessly pursue sexual pleasures and miss out on God's blessings. Discipline yourself and avoid strange women. Diligently guard your hearts and flee sexual immorality.

Don't be quick to open your zip and let down your pants. Pause and think! Wisdom and understanding will deaden the spirit of immorality in you, and cause you to live for God.

Delilah, Excuse Me!

The naïve young man does not understand the seriousness of sexual sin. He thinks of it as pleasure and so he accepts every invitation from every strange woman. He is soon led to his destruction. He seeks a second chance when it's too late already.

A sin may seem like one small seed, but the harvest of consequences are beyond measure. See what a single act of adultery brought David and Bathsheba. Amnon, David's firstborn raped Tamar, his half-sister, and was later murdered by Absalom in revenge. Absalom, David's third son, rebelled against David, and set up a tent on the roof (probably where David stood watching Bathsheba take her bath) and slept with ten of his father's concubines there. His pride led to his death. Adonijah, fourth son, set himself as king before David's death. His half-brother, Solomon, later had him executed. Solomon ironically had much grief because of his many wives just as his father. In fulfillment of God's punishment for David and Bathsheba's adultery, their unnamed son died on the seventh day after birth. "From this time on, your family will live by the sword because you have despised me by taking Uriah's wife to be your own. 'This is what the LORD says: Because of what you have done, I will cause your own household to rebel against you. I will give your wives to another man before your very eyes, and he will go to bed with them in public view. You did it secretly, but I will make this happen to you openly in the sight of all Israel' " (2 Samuel 12:10-12 NLT).

Bathsheba must have been devastated by the chain of events—unfaithfulness to her husband, discovery of pregnancy, death of her husband, and the death of her unnamed son.

The consequences of sin affect not only us but those we know and love. When Shechem raped Dinah, the consequences were far greater than he could have imagined. Dinah's brothers were outraged and took revenge. Pain, deceit, and murder followed.

Delilah, Excuse Me!

"And Dinah the daughter of Leah, which she bare unto Jacob, went out to see the daughters of the land.

And when Shechem the son of Hamor the Hivite, prince of the country, saw her, he took her, and lay with her, and defiled her."

"The sons of Jacob came upon the slain, and spoiled the city, because they had defiled their sister.

They took their sheep, and their oxen, and their asses, and that which was in the city, and that which was in the field,

And all their wealth, and all their little ones, and their wives took they captive, and spoiled even all that was in the house."

Genesis 34:1-2, 27-29

Sexual sin is devastating because its consequences are so far reaching.

What David did in secret was soon to be done by another in the open. What was private and confidential was soon to be made public. You would hear a public chorus of voices disapproving of the youth shamelessly publicizing sexual immorality. I think what the youth are doing is making public the private sins of the sexual immorality of the older generation. What David did secretly indoors became an outdoor game.

Zip up and live! Don't wait to see what will happen before you take heed to wisdom. Let your fountain be blessed. 'Why be captivated, my son, by an immoral woman, or fondle the breasts of a promiscuous woman?' Why spill the water of your springs in the streets, having sex with just anyone? It pays to wait, young man.

Switch: Renew Your Mind

Let God transform you into a new person by changing the way you think. "Throw off your old sinful nature and your former way of life, which is corrupted by lust and deception. Instead, let the Spirit renew your thoughts and attitudes" (Ephesians 4:22-23 NLT). You must switch! Forsake your old ways and pursue holiness. Let the strange women in your life know you're now a changed person; surprise them. Stay away from their path and doorway. Find new friends who are godly to help you switch.

Renew your mind; reconsider your thoughts. Ask yourself if Christ would think this way. Will Christ consider your thought as good or evil? If your thought wouldn't please Christ, then, switch. Think like Christ. Philippians 2:5 says, 'think the same way that Christ Jesus thought' (CEV). You need a spiritual renewal of your mind to stay pure in a world as this. The apostle Paul told young Timothy: "Run from anything that stimulates youthful lusts. Instead, pursue righteous living, faithfulness, love, and peace. Enjoy the companionship of those who call on the Lord with pure hearts" (2 Timothy 2:22 NLT).

Be careful what you think; your life is shaped by your thoughts. When there is a spiritual renewal of mind in you, your life is shaped to model Christ's.

Young Man, Cleanse Your Ways

To overcome sexual immorality you must change your mind about women. You must erase the picture of them as sex toys in your mind. Learn to see older women as mothers and younger women as sisters. Relate with younger women in all purity as you would your own sisters (1Timothy 5:2).

Renew your mind, young man. The women around you (especially those in the church) are not sex materials. They are fellow members in God's family. Protect them and help them grow spiritually.

Treat them as you would your family members. That's your responsibility. Do it and don't lust after them.

Finally, brethren, the Bible commends: "whatsoever things are true, whatsoever things are honest, whatsoever things are just, whatsoever things are pure, whatsoever things are lovely, whatsoever things are of good report; if there be any virtue, and if there be any praise, think on these things." I invite you to cancel every appointment with strange women and cross over to a life full of wisdom and understanding. Life void of wisdom and understating is naive. Get wisdom, get understanding: forget it not. "Wisdom is the principal thing; therefore get wisdom: and with all thy getting get understanding" (Proverbs 4:7), "that they may keep thee from the strange woman, from the stranger which flattereth with her words" (Proverbs 7:5).

Job 28:28 tells what *wisdom* and *understanding* really are: **"Behold, the fear of the Lord, that is wisdom; and to depart from evil is understanding."** Now that I've established the true meaning of the words wisdom and understanding as used in this book, let me crown my message with this good news.

Chapter Seven

GOOD NEWS

To evangelize is to spread the good news that Jesus Christ died for our sins and was raised from the dead according to the Scriptures, and that as the reigning Lord he now offers the forgiveness of sins and the liberating gift of the Spirit to all who repent and believe.

—John Stott

I'M no guru in matters of human sexuality; I do not pretend to be one either! Therefore, what I have in this book are not answers based on any human faculty to your sexuality problems. I do not wish, also, to provide you with any "How To" list of activities or training program to help manage your sexuality. What I however bring to light in this thought provoking book is the Good News as given me by God for every youth. My assignment would have been over if I presented to you the greatest Guru of all time—Jesus, the Son of the Living God. He alone can provide solution and cleansing to your messed-up sexual life. I therefore advise you to make a date with Him and your life will never be the same again!

It will be very good advice to have to tell you to abstain from sexual perversion. But my message will not be complete and adequate if all it does is give good advice, not only to virgin young men but also to my lovely brothers who for some reasons have, and are engaging in sexual perversion. In this case, it is like giving due warning as regards sexual perversion when it's rather too late! This book, therefore, is no good advice but Good News; Good News for every youth regardless of what they've

Good News

done or haven't done!

God still loves us as sinners. God hates sin not the sinner. That is why I choose to proclaim the good news which is the unlimited grace of God through Christ Jesus. He still loves you in spite of all your sins and is giving you today every opportunity and encouragement to repent. Whether you've been enticed by a strange woman or not, there's good news for you. Isn't it amazing to know that God's saving grace is by far greater than any sin man could ever commit?

How far have you gone? Jesus brought us good news, not good advice. It may be too late to bring you good advice, but never too late for the good news. Christ loved us and washed us from our sins with His own blood (Revelation 1:5). His love preceded His washing of us. He washed us from sin because He first loved us.

Paul in his struggle with the power of sin wrote: "For the good that I would I do not: but the evil which I would not, that I do. O wretched man that I am! who shall deliver me from the body of this death?" (Romans 7:19&24). There is none that does good, no not even one. But the love of Christ has qualified us all for His grace.

In Psalm 51, we read a psalm David wrote when Nathan the prophet came unto him, after he had gone in to Bathsheba. David's plea for mercy, forgiveness, and cleansing was accepted. Like David, we too can, and will be forgiven if we sincerely repent and turn from our sexual sins. No sin is too terrible or too great to be forgiven! God is merciful to those who truly feel sorry for their sins and repent (to change your mind). God loves you in spite of your sinful nature. He wants to help you come out of your sins. He hasn't given up on you yet. Whatever your mistakes, God will accept you just as you are and set you free from the load of sexual perversion. God always deals with us as we are today, now, not yesterday or years ago. He is faithful. He is merciful. So ask Him to help you now.

Dear God, I know that my sin has separated me from you. Thank you that Jesus Christ died in my place. I ask Jesus to forgive my sin and to come into my life. Please begin to direct my life. Show me the way out of sin and into the light of your freedom and your love. Thank you for giving me eternal life. In Jesus' name, Amen!

Young man, this is not just another of those books that seek to reprimand you, leaving you with no hope. It is that which will move and bless your heart, and not merely inform your mind. This book is a message from God full of heavenly wisdom and understanding to help you flee immorality, and to give you hope for a new life and a second chance to return and be made right with God. This book is a heavenly altar call: come home to Him, for that is good and is pleasing to Him and is perfect.

As you loosen yourself from the strange woman's grasp, please help your friends and loved ones do the same by sharing this Good News with them. You may want to send them copies of this book as gifts, or make your personal copy available to them. They would forever be thankful to you for saving them from the two edged sword of the strange woman.

I bring you this thought-provoking and challenging message, in obedience to the Holy Spirit, with passion and love and without self-righteousness. My dear friends in the Lord, now that we have received wisdom and understanding, let us boldly stand up to every strange woman; look them in the face and say, *Delilah, Excuse Me!*

ABOUT THE AUTHOR

JOSEPH Sayibu is a former laity in-charge of the Dunamis Assemblies of God Church, Zabzugu – Ghana.

He has over the years served in various Christian leadership roles. Notably among them are local chapter President of the Assemblies of God Campus Ministry (AGCM), both in Senior High School and in College. He also served as the Evangelism and Missions Secretary of the Nurses' Christian Fellowship (NCF) in College. During these years he preached and taught the Word of God on campus.

He is motivated by a desire to reach out to the world with the supremely valuable message of Salvation in Jesus Christ. You would hear him say, *"I might not have a giant pulpit to myself but I'm not ruled out. I must fulfil my part of the Great Commission!"*

He is currently a medical student in China, and serving with the Bible Study and Sunday School Department of Jinzhou International Christian Fellowship (JICF).